A GRAMMAR
OF THE
BHOTANTA, OR BOUTAN LANGUAGE

A GRAMMAR
OF THE
BHOTANTA, OR BOUTAN LANGUAGE

REV. FREDERIC CHRISTIAN G. SCHRCETER

EDITED BY
W. CAREY

GYAN

Published by

Gyan Publishing House
5, Ansari Road
Daryaganj, New Delhi-110002
Phone: 011-47034999, 9811692060
E-mail: books@gyanbooks.com

Distribution Network
gyanbooks.com
India, USA, Canada, UK, Australia, France

ISBN : 978-81-212-4389-6 (PB)
First Published, Serampore 1826

2nd Impression 2020

Printed at: Gyan Press, Delhi.

A Grammar of the Bhotanta, or Boutan Language
Author: Rev. Frederic Christian G. Schrceter

DICTIONARY

OF THE

Bhotanta, or Boutan Language,

PRINTED FROM A MANUSCRIPT COPY

MADE BY

THE LATE REV. FREDERIC CHRISTIAN GOTTHELF SCHRŒTER,

EDITED BY JOHN MARSHMAN.

TO WHICH IS PREFIXED

A GRAMMAR

OF THE

BHOTANTA LANGUAGE.

BY FREDERIC CHRISTIAN GOTTHELF SCHRŒTER.

EDITED BY W. CAREY, D. D. F. L. S. F. G. S.

SERAMPORE:

1826.

PREFACE.

THE work now presented to the public consists of a Grammar, and Dictionary of the language of Thibet and Bhot*a*, more frequently written Bhotant*a*, but called Boutan by Europeans. This, however, is not only the language of Thibet and Boutan, but is also ascertained to be the language of little Thibet; and as these countries are a thousand miles distant from each other, it is inferred that this language is spoken throughout the whole of the region on the summit of the H*i*mal*u*y*a* mountains, usually called Chinese Tartary, and some other countries bordering thereon, all of which are mostly, if not altogether under the dominion or influence of China, and occupy the space between the English and the Russian possessions.

In a political point of view, a knowledge of the countries bordering on our own territories, and of the languages spoken in them, is of great importance, as furnishing facilities for friendly intercourse with the people who inhabit them, and opening to us all the commerical advantages which those countries afford: while, at the same time, it affords equal facilities for discovering hostile intentions when they exist, and furnishes an intelligible medium of negociation with the people.

The mutual affinities of different languages will always be considered important by those who study human nature, as conducting us to some of the most rational conclusions respecting the relations of the different nations of the earth to each other. The labours of philologists have thrown much light on things connected with this subject which are in their nature exceedingly obscure, and by opening the way to a knowledge of the religion, the philosophy, the jurisprudence, and the popular customs of different nations have presented a wide and highly interesting field to the view of those who study the history of their species.

Most of the languages spoken on the earth may be placed in certain classes, perhaps few in number, at the head of each of which stands the language which is accounted the parent of the rest. All the Indian languages, for instance, are confessedly derived from the S*u*ngskr*i*ta, the Arabic and its congeners from Hebrew; the Greek, the Latin, the Teutonic, the Sclavonic, and perhaps the Chinese will also stand at the head of their respective classes. It is highly probable that equally strong affinities exist between many of the Tartar languages, and perhaps also, between the different languages of Africa, and those of the American Indians, which, however, yet remain to be distinguished from each other, and classically arranged, before the relations of the different classes of those languages, with those spoken in other parts of the world, can be traced out.

There is a more than ordinary importance in the languages which form the extreme limits of each class; the foreign words introduced into these bordering dialects, or the corruption of words from their original form, if accurately marked, would prove a highly interesting subject and lead to important results. In this point of view the language of Boutan must be of the first importance as it occupies a line of a thousand miles, or more, of border land between the languages of India, derived from the S*u*ngskr*i*ta, and the languages spoken throughout Russian and independent Tartary, of which, at present, we know very little.

It is highly probable that the following Dictionary was written by some of the Roman Catholic missionaries who formerly laboured in Thibet. A copy of it was in the possession of the late Major Latter, which was copied by the late Rev. Mr. Schrœter, a missionary belonging to the Church Missionary Society. Mr. Schrœter was placed at Tental*i*ya, a military post in Poornea, and received a salary from Government. On his demise his Manuscripts were submitted to the inspection of the editor, and at his recommendation, the printing of the whole was sanctioned by Government, and the expense supported by a generous subscription.

The Dictionary was originally written in Italian, and has been partly translated into English by Mr. Marshman. Some few words, the explanation of which was very obscure, are marked with a *.—The arrangement is that of the Alphabet, as exhibited in the Grammar, with this exception that the letters of the third class, which are very few, are mixed with those of the second, and must be sought for among them. This was not observed till the printing was too far advanced to remedy it, without reprinting the whole of the words beginning with the letters of these two classes; and as the words are very few, and the inconvenience scarcely perceptible, it was not thought an object of sufficient magnitude to warrant the reprint.

The Grammar is very short, and deficient in some important points; but it is all that Mr. Schrœter had written. The editor therefore did not think himself warranted in attempting any additions; and, indeed, his knowledge of the Boutan language is too slight to admit of it. It is therefore given to the public as left by its author, those few verbal alterations excepted, which the author's imperfect knowledge of the English language rendered necessary.

W. CAREY.

A

GRAMMAR

OF

The Bhotan Language.

SECTION I.

Of the mode of writing, and the signs.

THE Tibetians use two kinds of characters, one, they denominate (དབུ་ཅན་) Oo-chen, which signifies *headed*, or *having a head*; *e. g.* ཀ་ ཁ་ ག་ ང་, &c.; the other is called (དབུ་མེད་) Oo-medh, which signifies *having no head*; *e. g.* ཀ། ཁ། ག། ང།, &c.

The characters called དབུ་ཅན། Oo-chen are used chiefly in their sacred writings, and other printed works; but the other kind called དབུ་མེད་ Oo-medh, in correspondence or for business. There is no difference between them beside that of form, the sound of the characters is the same in both, and both Alphabets run parallel with each other. The Tibetians use various signs in their writings and books, which have no meaning in themselves, but are placed either at the beginning of a work, or page, or at the beginning and end of a sentence, or between each syllable, and at the end of a work. Those placed at the beginning of a work are most generally the following: ༄༅། ༄༅༔ ༄༔ ༄།

Those at the end of a sentence are such as follow: *e. g.* །༔འབྲུག་སྐད་ཏུ༔, Bhoke-dhoo, *in the language of Bhotan*; or ། རྒྱ་གར་སྐད་ཏུ།, Gya-ghar-ko-dhoo, *in the language of Bengal*; and when the subject is quite finished, two perpendicular strokes are put, as ༎. The syllables are divided by a point (་) as will be seen in the following line: ཆུའི་ཕ་རོལ་ཏུ་འདོ། chhooi-pha-rol-dhoo-do, *Go beyond the river or water;* but at the end of a work every author or writer makes a mark according to his own fancy; perhaps in this manner ། ° ° ° ° ° ། ༎ ~ ༎.

SECTION II.

Of the Consonants.

We now proceed to the Alphabet; and as the characters called དབུ་ཅན་, Oo-chen, are most employed in printed works, and are read with greater ease, it will be proper to take that form in preference to the other. The Tibetian Alphabet consists of thirty consonants, and four signs for vowels. The consonants are called ཀ་མ་ kama, and are divided into eight classes, each class having four letters, the latter excepted, which has only two. Every consonant has its inherent vowel a, and is thus capable of forming a syllable of itself; for instance: ཉ nya, *a fish*; ཁ་ kha, *the mouth*; ས sa, *the earth*. Besides this, the Tibetians have also an artificial way of making letters, by placing different consonants either above or near each other, which they are under the necessity of doing to produce sounds not directly in their alphabetical system, and also to distinguish things and words in writing from each other, which in speaking are denoted by the same sound, as we shall see hereafter. The thirty consonants are written in the following order. In reading, pronounce the inherent vowel as a in half, craft, &c.

༄༅། ཀ་	ཁ་	ག་	ང་
ka	kha	gha	nga
ཅ་	ཆ་	ཇ་	ཉ།
cha	chha	jha	nya
ཏ་	ཐ་	ད་	ན།
ta	tha	dha	na
པ་	ཕ་	བ་	མ།
pa	pha	bha	ma

ཙ་	ཚ་	ཛ་	ཝ།
tsa	tsha	dsha	wa
ཞ་	ཟ་	འ་	ཡ་
sha	sa	a	ya
ར་	ལ་	ཤ་	ས་
ra	la	sha	sa
	ཧ་	ཨ་།།	
	ha	a	

Five of these letters, namely, the third of each of the first five classes: ག་ ཇ་ ད་ བ་ ཛ་ change their sound; for the Tibetians, having no signs for g, j, d, b, and dsa, in their alphabetical system, supply their place by the following position of letters:

དགའ་	མགའ་	འགའ་	རྒ་	ལྒ་	སྒ་།
ga	ga	ga	ga	ga	ga
འཇའ་	མཇའ་	རྗ	ལྗ		
ja.	ja	ja	ja		
བདའ་	མདའ་	འདའ་	རྡ་	ལྡ་	སྡ་།
da	da	da	da	da	da
འབལ་	སྦ་	རྦ་	ལྦ་།		
ba	ba	ba	ba or wa		
འཛའ་	མཛའ་	རྫ་	ལྫ་།		
dsa	dsa	dsa	dsa		

Hear the reader must be cautioned not to confound the syllables དགའ་ མགའ བདའ་ མདའ་ with དག་ མག་ བད་ མད་ for these consisting only of two consonants, are read dhagh, magh, bhá, má; it must be understood, that ག་ gha, and ད dha become g and d, only in syllables of three cosonants, or of two consonants with a vowel, *e. g.* དགའ་ བ་ gawa, *joy;* དགེ་ བ་ gewa, *virtue, piety;* མགའ་ ga, མགོ go, *the head;* འདའ་ da, བདེ་པ depa, *peace;* མདའ da, *an arrow;* མདོ do, *a kind of book:* with regard to the rest no mistake can occur.

Five consonants, viz. ག་ ད་ བ་ མ་ འ་ are frequently mute at the beginning of a word or syllable; ད་ and ས་ are mute at the end of a word or syllable; and ད་ ན་ ས་ have the power of changing the preceding vowel into a diphthong. This will be more fully explained in treating of each letter separately.

SECTION III.

Of the Vowels.

Besides the vowel a, which is inherent in every consonant, four other vowels, called by the Tibetians ཡན་ ལག་ yon-lagh, or དབྱངས་ཡིག། the first word signifying *a member* or *joint;* the second *singing* or *sounding letters*, the signs and names used for them in spelling are the following:

Name.	*Shape.*	*Power.*
ཀི་གུ་། ki-koo	ི	*i* as in will
འགྲེང་བུ། deng-bhoo	ེ	e in ell
ཞབས་ཀྱུ། shabh-choo	ུ	*oo* in good
ན་རོ་། na-ro	ོ	o in robe

The first, second, and fourth of these vowels are placed above the consonant, and the third beneath it; for instance: ཀི་ k*i*, ཀེ་ ke, ཀུ་ k̲oo, ཀོ་ ko, &c.

To make these vowels long, འ is put underneath the consonant, and then they stand thus:

ཨ	ཨཱ	ཨི	ཨཱི	ཨེ	ཨཻ	ཨུ	ཨཱུ
a	â	*i*	ee	e	i	*oo*	oo
ཨོ	ཨཽ	རྀ	རཱྀ	ལྀ	ལཱྀ	ཨཾ	ཨཱཿ
o	ô	r*i*	ree	l*i*	lee	am	ah

When connected with consonants, they are read in the following manner:

ཀ་	ཀཱ་	ཀི་	ཀཱི་	ཀེ་	ཀཻ་
ka	kâ	k*i*	kee	ke	ki

ཀུ་	ཀཱུ	ཀོ་	ཀཽ་	ཀཾ་	ཀཿ or ཀ་ཁས།
koo	k̄oo	ko	kô	kam	ka kah

Sometimes the vowels are placed double above each other and then they are pronounced as a long vowel; but it is more frequently the case that they denote an abbreviation of the word, so that the reader ought to make two syllables of it, as we shall see hereafter among the abbreviations. Sometimes the vowel *i* is placed over a letter in an opposite direction to that above mentioned, for instance: ཀྀ་ཁྀ་ངྀ་, &c. but though the shape is altered the sound is the same; it is used to express the S*u*ngskr*i*t*a* ཪ.

SECTION IV.

The combination of the Vowels with the Consonants.

To show the combination of the vowels with the consonants more fully, and to facilitate thereby the reading of the language, the Tibetians make thirty sections or classes of the thirty consonants combined with the vowels, and exhibit them in the following manner:

༄༅།། ཀི	ཀེ	ཀུ	ཀོན།	ཉི	ཉེ	ཉུ	ཉོན།
k*i*	ke	k*oo*	kön	ny*i*	nye	ny*oo*	nyön
ཁི	ཁེ	ཁུ	ཁོམས།	ཏི	ཏེ	ཏུ	ཏོག།
kh*i*	khe	kh*oo*	khom	t*i*	te	t*oo*	togh
གི	གེ	གུ	གོར།	ཐི	ཐེ	ཐུ	ཐོབ།
gh*i*	ghe	gh*oo*	ghor	th*i*	the	th*oo*	thobh
ངི	ངེ	ངུ	ངོར།	དི	དེ	དུ	དོན།
ng*i*	nge	ng*oo*	ngor	dh*i*	dhe	dh*oo*	dhon
ཅི	ཅེ	ཅུ	ཅོལ།	ནི	ནེ	ནུ	ནོར།
ch*i*	che	ch*oo*	chol	n*i*	ne	n*oo*	nor
ཆི	ཆེ	ཆུ	ཆོས།	པི	པེ	པུ	པོངས།
chh*i*	chhe	chh*oo*	chhö	p*i*	pe	p*oo*	pong
ཇི	ཇེ	ཇུ	ཇོན།	ཕི	ཕེ	ཕུ	ཕོས།
jh*i*	jhe	jh*oo*	jhön	ph*i*	phe	ph*oo*	phö

བི	བེ	བུ	བོན།	འི	འེ	འུ	འོར།
bhi	bhe	bhoo	bhön	i	e	oo	or
མི	མེ	མུ	མོན།	ཡི	ཡེ	ཡུ	ཡོངས།
mi	me	moo	mön	yi	ye	yoo	yong
ཙི	ཙེ	ཙུ	ཙོན།	རི	རེ	རུ	རོལ།
tsi	tse	tsoo	tsön	ri	re	roo	rol
ཚི	ཚེ	ཚུ	ཚོལ།	ལི	ལེ	ལུ	ལོག།
tshi	tshe	tshoo	tshol	li	le	loo	logh
ཛི	ཛེ	ཛུ	ཛོམ།	ཤི	ཤེ	ཤུ	ཤོག།
dshi	dshe	dshoo	dshom	shi	she	shoo	shogh
ཝི	ཝེ	ཝུ	ཝོལ།	སི	སེ	སུ	སོལ།
wi	we	woo	wol	si	se	soo	sol
ཞི	ཞེ	ཞུ	ཞོན།	ཧི	ཧེ	ཧུ	ཧོར།
shi	she	shoo	shön	hi	he	hoo	hor
ཟི	ཟེ	ཟུ	ཟོངས	ཨི	ཨེ	ཨུ	ཨོམ།
si	se	sho.	song	i	e	oo	om

In the above table the fourth or last letter of the series has always another put after it, so as to form a syllable ending in a consonant; this is done to accustom the scholar to the method of reading, to show him how to form syllables, and to teach him at the same time that the consonant at the end of a syllable loses its inherent vowel; for instance, ཀོན kon is not to be read kona, but kon; ཁོམས khom is not to be read khoma, but khom;* གོར ghor is not to be read ghora, but ghor, &c.

Sometimes a consonant has two vowels, one beneath, and one above. *Exam.* བཅིུག་. When this is the case it is always an abbreviation of two syllables; the Example given must be read བཅུ་གཅིག choo-chigh, *eleven.*

When a double consonant ends a syllable, both the upper and lower consonant is pronounced; for instance: སངྐ sangka, which is not read sank, but sangka; upon the same principle read ཤཱསྟྲ shastra, ཀུནྡའི koondai, སམ་བྷོཊ་ sambhota,† འཇིགྲྟེན་ jigten, &c.

* ག at the end of a word or syllable is always mute, as mentioned before.

† The name of the author of the book called ཟ་མ་ཏོག་བཀོད་པ།.

SECTION V.

On Pronunciation.

Before we proceed to those characters which are compounded with yata and rata it is necessary to lay down a common rule for the pronunciation of each letter separately.

ཀ་ ka, is pronounced as k in king. This letter is mute when written over ལ la, as in ཀླ la.

ཁ kha, is pronounced as *kh* in blac*k h*orse.

ག་ gha, as *gh* in lo*g-h*ouse. This letter is the first of those, which lose their power and change their sound: as particularized below. See also page 3.

1. ག་ gha having ད་ dha, འ་ a, or མ་ ma, prefixed, or ར་ ra, ལ་ la, or ས་ sa placed over it, is pronounced as g in give.

2. ག་ gha without a vowel either above or underneath it, at the beginning of a syllable consisting of three or more consonants, is mute, when prefixed to the following eleven letters, ཅ་ ཉ་ ཏ་ ད་ ན་ ཙ་ ཞ་ ཟ་ ཡ་ ཤ་ ས་. Hence read གཅའ cha, གཉའ nya, གཏའ ta, གདའ dadh, གནའ na, གཙོའ tsa, གཞའ sha, གཟའ sa, གཡའ ya, གཤའ sha, གསའ sa.

3. ག་ gha, is mute over ལ་ la, as in གླ་ la.

4. If a word or syllable terminate in ག་ gha, it is pronounced, but if in གས་ it is mute, these two letters being written for the sign (:) called in the Sungskrita language visurga. Hence read གསེག་མ་ seghma, *a breach*, but གཟུགས་ sooh, *shape, a body*.

ང་ gna, a nasal sound.

ཅ་ cha, is sounded as ch in church.

ཆ་ chha, has the sound of *chh* in coa*ch-h*ouse.

ཇ་ jha, is j aspirated. This is the second letter which loses its power, it is however never mute. When འ་ a, or མ་ ma, are prefixed, or ར་ ra, or ལ་ la, placed on the head of it, it is pronounced as j in judge. See also page 3.

ཉ་ nya, a nasal sound.

ཏ་ ta, is the dental t.

ཐ་ tha, the last letter, sensibly aspirated.

ད་ dha, the dental d aspirated. This letter is the third that changes its sound; and loses its power, as particularised below. Sec also page 3.

1. ད་ dha having བ་ bha, མ་ ma, or འ a, prefixed, or ར་ ra, ལ་ la, or ས་ sa, placed on the top of it, becomes the unaspirated d. Hence read the following: འད་ da, བད་ da, མད་ da, རྡ་ da, ལྡ་ da, སྡ་ da.

2. ད་ dha, without a vowel either above or underneath it, at the beginning of a syllable consisting of three or more consonants, is mute when prefixed to the following six letters; ཀ་ ག་ ང་ པ་ བ་ མ་. Hence read: དཀའ་ ka, དགའ་ ga, དངའ་ nga, དཔའ་ pa, དབའ་ ba, དམའ་ ma.

3. ད་ dha at the end of a syllable has the power of changing the preceding vowels, namely, the inherent vowel a into â, as pronounced in the word mare; ུ *oo* into the French u or German ü, and ོ o, into the French eu or German ö.* *Exam.* ཚད་ is not read tshadh as it regularly would be, but tshâ or tshâdh; ཆུད་པ། is not read chhoodh-pa, but chhü-pa or chhüdh-pa; ཤོད is not read shodh, but shö or shödh.

* Those unacquainted with the exact sound of these foreign diphthongs had better read the oo and unaltered.

ན་ na, is pronounced like the English n. At the end of a word or syllable it has the same effect as the preceding ད་ dha; viz. it occasions the preceding vowels to be changed into diphthongs, namely, ུ into the French u or German ü, ོ into the French eu or German ö, and the inherent vowel into â, pronounced like a in mare. It never changes its sound, and is never mute. *Exam.* ཕུན་ is not read phoon as it regularly would be, but as phün; པོན་ is not read pon but pön; ངན་ is not read ngan but ngân.

པ་ pa, has the sound of the English p.

ཕ་ pha, is pronounced as p with an aspiration, sensibly, though closely expressed as one letter only.

བ་ bha, is b with an aspiration. This letter is the fourth which changes its sound and loses its power.

1. བ་ bha having འ་ prefixed or ར་ ra, ལ་ la, ས་ sa, placed over it, loses its proper sound and is pronounced as the English b.

2. བ་ bha, without a vowel either above or underneath it, at the beginning of a word or syllable consisting of three or more letters, is mute when prefixed to the following ten letters: ཀ་ ག་ ཅ་ ཏ་ ད་ ཙ་ ཞ་ ཟ་ ཤ་ ས་. *Exam.* བཀའ་ ka, བགའ་ ga, བཅའ་ ha, བཏའ་ ta, བདའ་ da, བཙའ་ tsa, བཞའ་ sha, བཟའ་ sa, བཤའ་ sha, བསའ་ sa.

3. བ་ bha, is never mute at the end of a syllable or word, but it is mute when it stands above another letter, or is the first member of a compound letter: *e. g.* བློ་ lo, *the mind;* བླ་མ་ lama, *a priest, a spiritual teacher.*

4. བ་ bha, is often written for ཝ་ wa, especially when it is the termination of the infinitive, and then it is pronounced as w; for instance, འགྲོ་བ་ da-wa, *to go;* it is also pronounced wa after the letters ང་ འ་ ར་ ལ་།

5. བ་ bha, with ད་ dha prefixed, becomes wa, as in དབང་ wang, *a king, or ru-*

ler. It is also used in the same manner as འ and becomes mute as in དབུ་ oo, *a head;* དབུལ་ ool, *poor, low, mean.* In this case it serves only as a head to the vowel.

མ་ ma, is sounded as the English m.

1. མ་ ma, without a vowel above or beneath it, at the beginning of a syllable consisting of three or more letters, is mute when prefixed to the following eleven letters: ཁ་ ག་ ང་ ཆ་ ཇ་ ཉ་ ཐ་ ད་ ན་ ཚ་ ཛ་. *Exam.* མཁའ་ kha, མགའ་ ga, མངའ་ nga, མཆའ་ chha, མཇའ་ ja, མཉའ་ nya, མཐའ་ tha, མདའ་ da, མནའ་ na, མཚའ་ tsha, མཛའ་ dsa.

2. When prefixed to ག་ gha, ད་ dha, ཇ་ jha, ཛ་ dsha, it causes them to become unaspirated.

3. It is represented by a small round circle ॰, written over the letter, for instance in སྐོཾ kom, *dry;* རྣཾས་ nam, *all;* ཐཾས་ཅད། tham-che, *all;* or ཐཾས་ཅད་ tham-che, *all;* these words would otherwise be written སྐོམ་ kom, རྣམས་ nam, ཐམས་ཅད་ tham-che.

ཙ་ tsa, a sound which cannot be expressed in the English tongue by a single letter.

ཚ་ tsha, the former aspirated.

ཛ་ dsha, a sound not existing in the English tongue. When འ་ a, or མ་ ma, is prefixed, or ར་ ra, or ལ་ la, placed over this letter, it loses its aspiration and becomes dsa.

ཝ་ wa, has the sound of the English w.

ཞ་ sha, ཟ་ sa, have a hollow sound strongly pronounced in the throat.

ཟ་ sa, placed over ལ་ la, is pronounced ཟླ་ da, as in ཟླ་བ dawa, *the moon.*

འ་ a, has a deep guttural sound like ཞ་ and ཟ་.

1. འ་ prefixed to ག་ gha, ད་ dha, ཇ་ jha, ཛ་ dsha, occasions them to become unaspirated.

2. This letter without a vowel either above or beneath it, at the beginning of a syllable consisting of three or more letters, is mute when prefixed to the following ten letters : ཁ་ ག་ ཆ་ ཇ་ ཐ་ ད་ ཕ་ བ་ ཚ་ ཛ་. *Exam.* འཁའ་ kha, འགའ་ ga, འཆའ་ chha, འཇའ་ ja, འཐའ་ tha, འདའ་ da, འཕའ་ pha, འབའ་ ba, འཚའ་ tsha, འཛའ་ dsa.

ཡ་ ya, has the sound of the English y in yoke. This letter is often compounded with a preceding consonant and its powers when thus compounded will be treated of in the next Section.

ར་ has the sound of the English r. It is always mute when placed over the following twelve letters: ཀ་ ག་ ང་ ཇ་ ཉ་ ཏ་ ད་ ན་ བ་ མ་ ཙ་ ཛ་ *Exam.* རྐ་ ka, རྒ་ ga, རྔ་ nga, རྗ་ ja, རྙ་ nya, རྟ་ ta, རྡ་ da, རྣ་ na, རྦ་ ba, རྨ་ ma, རྩ་ tsa, རྫ་ dsa.

ལ་ la, has the power of the English l. It is always mute at the top of the following letters: ཀ་ ག་ ང་ ཅ་ ཇ་ ཏ་ ད་ པ་ བ་. *Exam.* ལྐ་ ka, ལྒ་ ga, ལྔ་ nga, ལྕ་ cha, ལྗ་ ja, ལྟ་ ta, ལྡ་ da, ལྤ་ pa, ལྦ་ ba, or wa.

ལ་ la, written at the foot of ཟ་, becomes da; hence read ཟླ་བ། dawa, *the moon;* when placed over ཧ་ it is written and pronounced ལྷ་ lha.

ཤ་ sha, has the sound of the English sh.

ས་ sa, is pronounced like s in sin. It is always mute when written at the top of the following twelve letters: ཀ་ ག་ ང་ ཉ་ ཏ་ ད་ ན་ པ་ བ་ མ་ ཙ་ ལ་. *Exam.* སྐ་ ka, སྒ་ ga, སྔ་ nga, སྙ་ nya, སྟ་ ta, སྡ་ da, སྣ་ na, སྤ་ pa, སྦ་ ba, སྨ་ ma, སྩ་ tsa, སླ་ la.

ས་ sa, like ད་ dha, and ན་ na, occasions the change of the preceding vowels into diphthongs, making ུ oo take the sound of the French u or German ü, and ོ o, that of the French eu or German ö; and the inherent vowel a that of a in mare ; the ས་ is then always mute. *Exam.* དུས་ is not pronounced dhoo, but dhu; ཆོས་ is not pronounced chho, but chhö; ཟས་ is not pronounced sa, but sá.

ཧ ha, has the power of h in the English word horse.

ཨ་ a, as a in father.

SECTION VI.

Of the signs Yata and Rata.

The letters ཡ་ and ར་ ra, in a different form, are frequently joined with a preceding consonant to form compound letters, and are placed at the foot of the other consonant; the first is called ཡ་བཏགས་ Yata, and has this form ྱ; the other is called ར་བཏགས་ Rata, and is written thus ྲ. They both occasion the consonants under which they are placed to alter their original sound, and either give them an additional power, or change them altogether.

The sign ྱ yata is a symbol to represent the letter ཡ་ ya, and has the same power. Yata may be annexed to the following eight letters: ཀ་ ka, ཁ་ kha, ག་ gha, པ་ pa, ཕ་ pha, བ་ bha, མ་ ma, ར་ ra. *Exam.* ཀྱ་ kya, ཁྱ་ kh'ya, གྱ་ gh'ya, པྱ་ cha, ཕྱ་ chya, བྱ་ jhya, མྱ, nya, རྱ་ ya.

ཀྱ་ kya, is sometimes though seldom pronounced cha as the English ch in church: the mute letters ར་ ra, ས་ sa may be placed over it, when it is written thus: རྐྱ་ kya, སྐྱ་ kya.

ཁྱ་ khya is sometimes pronounced ཆ་ chha, as in the pronoun ཁྱོད་ khyo, *you*, which may be read khyo and chho.

གྱ་ ghya, is sometimes pronounced jha. What has been said in the rules (See page 7.) concerning the letter ག་ gha, is applicable here also, viz. གྱ་ gh'ya with ད་ dha, འ་ a, མ་ ma, prefixed, or ར་ ra, ལ་ la, ས་ sa, placed over it, becomes gya. *Exam.* དགྱ་ gya, མགྱ་ gya, འགྱ་ gya, རྒྱ་ gya, ལྒྱ་ gya, སྒྱ་ gya.

པྱ་ cha, and ཕྱ་ chha are not altered in sound by yata but have the same power with ཅ་ cha, ཆ་ chha. When the mute letter ས་ is placed over them, they are written thus, སྤྱ་ cha, སྥྱ་ chha.

བྱ་ jha, has the same sound as ཇ་ jha. What has been said (page 9.) relating to the letter བ་ bha, is partly applicable here also.

1. If འ་ be prefixed to, or the mute letter ས་ be placed over this letter, it loses its aspiration and is pronounced as the English j in judge. *Exam.* འབྱ་ ja, སྦྱ་ ja.

2. བྱ་ jha, becomes དབྱ་ ya, when ད་ dha, is prefixed to it, and is then pronounced as the letter ཡ་ ya, or the English y in you. *Exam.* དབྱིངས་ ying, *height;* དབྱངས་པ་ yang-pa, *to float;* དབྱེ་བ་ ye-wa, *to open.*

These compound letters admit all the vowels to be placed above and beneath them, in the same manner as the simple ones. The following syllables will serve as a specimen.

ཀྱི་ ky*i*	ཀྱེ་ kye	ཀྱུ་ ky*oo*	ཀྱོ་ kyo	ཀྱན་ kyen	ཀྱས་ kye	ཀྱོམ་ kyom	ཀྱུན་ khyüm
ཁྱི་ khy*i*	ཁྱེ་ khye	ཁྱུ་ khy*oo*	ཁྱོ་ khyo	ཁྱིས་ khy*i*	ཁྱེས khye	ཁྱོག་ khyogh	ཁྱུལ་ khy*oo*l
གྱི་ ghy*i*	གྱེ་ ghye	གྱུ་ ghy*oo*	གྱོ་ ghyo	གྱིམ་ ghy*i*m	གྱེན་ ghyen	གྱོད་ ghyodh	གྱུན་ ghyün
སྤྱི་ ch*i*	སྤྱེ་ che	སྤྱུ་ ch*oo*	སྤྱོ cho	པྱག་ chagh	པྱའ་ cha	པྱན་ chen	པྱུབ་ ch*oo*bh
ཕྱི་ chh*i*	ཕྱེ་ chhe	ཕྱུ་ chh*oo*	ཕྱོ་ chho	ཕྱར་ chhar	ཕྱམ་ chham	ཕྱད་ chhe	ཕྱོབ་ chhobh
བྱི་ jh*i*	བྱེ་ jhe	བྱུ་ jh*oo*	བྱོ་ jho	བྱས་ jhe	བྱིན་ jh*i*n	བྱོམ་ jhom	བྱུངས་ jh*oo*ng
མྱི་ ny*i*	མྱེ་ nye	མྱུ ny*oo*	མྱོ་ nyo	མྱག་ nyagh	མྱུར་ ny*oo*r	མྱལ་ nyel	མྱོད་ nyödh
ཡི་ y*i*	ཡེ་ ye	ཡུ་ y*oo*	ཡོ་ yo	ཡོས་ yö	ཡེན་ yen	ཡེད་ yedh	ཡུམ་ y*oo*m

The sign ྲ Rata is the representative symbol of ར་ ra, and is placed at the foot of the consonant. It is used to give to some consonants an additional sound, and to change others entirely. The letters under which the sign Rata may be written are the following fourteen :

ཀ་	ཁ་	ག་	ཏ་	ཐ་	ད་	ན་
ka	kha	gha	ta	tha	dha	na
པ་	ཕ་	བ་	མ་	ཤ་	ས་	ཧ་
pa	pha	bha	ma	sha	sa	ha

Which, Rata being subjoined to them, have the following appearance and sounds:

ཀྲ་	ཁྲ་	གྲ་	ཏྲ་	ཐྲ་	དྲ	ནྲ
ta	tha	dha	ta	tha	dha	nra
པྲ་	ཕྲ་	བྲ་	མྲ་	ཤྲ་	སྲ་	ཧྲ་
ta	tha	dha	mra	shra	sra	hra

Observe the following remarks :

ཀྲ་ ཏྲ་ པྲ་ sound almost like the English t; they agree with the Bengalee ট, or Nag*u*ree ट.

ཁྲ་ ཐྲ་ ཕྲ sound almost like the English t aspirated; they agree with the Bengalee ঠ or Nag*u*ree ठ.

གྲ་ དྲ་ བྲ་ sound almost like the English d aspirated ; they agree with the Bengalee ঢ or Nag*u*ree ढ. But གྲ་ dha loses its aspiration when the mute letters ད dha, འ a, མ ma, are prefixed to it, or ས be placed over it. *Exam.* དགྲ་ da, འགྲ་ da, མགྲ་ da, སྒྲ་ da. In the same manner དྲ and བྲ become unaspirated, when any of the mute letters are prefixed to, or placed on the top of them.

These compound letters admit all the vowels like simple letters, as may be seen from reading the following syllables:

ཀྲི་	ཀྲེ་	ཀྲུ་	ཀྲོ་	ཀྲིམ་	ཀྲུས་	ཀྲེན་	ཀྲོལ་
ti	te	*too*	to	*tim*	tu	ten	tol
ཁྲི་	ཁྲེ་	ཁྲུ་	ཁྲོ་	ཁྲིག་	ཁྲེལ་	ཁྲུས་	ཁྲོམ་
t'h*i*	t'he	t'h*oo*	t'ho	th*i*gh	thel	thü	thom
གྲི་	གྲེ་	གྲུ་	གྲོ་	གྲེས་	གྲམ་	གྲུབ་	གྲོམས་
dh*i*	dhe	dh*oo*	dho	dhe	dham	dh*oo*bh	d'hom
ཏྲི་	ཏྲེ་	ཏྲུ་	ཏྲོ་	ཏྲིག་	ཏྲེན་	ཏྲུམ་	ཏྲོས་
t*i*	te	*too*	to	t*i*gh	ten	t*oo*m	to
ཐྲི་	ཐྲེ་	ཐྲུ་	ཐྲོ་	ཐྲན་	ཐྲིམ་	ཐྲེའུ་	ཐྲང་
th*i*	the	th*oo*	tho	then	thom	the	thang
དྲི་	དྲེ་	དྲུ་	དྲོ་	དྲོས་	དྲེམ་	དྲུག་	དྲིལ་
dh*i*	dhe	dh*oo*	dho	dhö	dhem	dh*oo*gh	dh*i*l
ནྲི་	ནྲེ་	ནྲུ་	ནྲོ་	ནྲག་	ནྲུམ་	ནྲར་	ནྲོལ་
nr*i*	nre	nr*oo*	nro	nragh	nrum	nre	nrol
པྲི་	པྲེ་	པྲུ་	པྲོ་	པྲོས་	པྲེལ་	པྲིར་	པྲུན་
t*i*	te	*too*	to	tö	tel	*ti*	tün
ཕྲི་	ཕྲེ་	ཕྲུ་	ཕྲོ་	ཕྲག་	ཕྲེན་	ཕྲུལ་	ཕྲིང་
th*i*	the	th*oo*	tho	thagh	then	th*oo*l	thi
བྲི་	བྲེ་	བྲུ་	བྲོ་	བྲེས་	བྲུལ་	བྲིན་	བྲོམ་
dh*i*	dhe	dh*oo*	dho	dhe	dh*oo*l	dh*i*n	dhom
མྲི	མྲེ་	མྲུ་	མྲོ་	མྲེས་	མྲིན་	མྲོས་	མྲུལ་
mr*i*	mre	mr*oo*	mro	mr*i*	mre	mro	mr*oo*l
ཤྲི་	ཤྲེ་	ཤྲུ་	ཤྲོ་	ཤྲག་	ཤྲུན་	ཤྲེར་	ཤྲོམ་
shr*i*	shre	shr*oo*	shro	shragh	shrün	shre	shr*oo*m
སྲི་	སྲེ་	སྲུ་	སྲོ་	སྲའ་	སྲུན་	སྲེབ་	སྲོམ་
hr*i*	hre	hr*oo*	hro	sra	srün	sre	srom
ཧྲི་	ཧྲེ་	ཧྲུ་	ཧྲོ་	ཧྲིམ་	ཧྲུས་	ཧྲེན་	ཧྲོལ་
hr*i*	hre	hr*oo*	hro	hr*i*m	hru	hren	hrol

The letter ཝ་ in the form of a triangle is also placed at the foot of letters; it has the sound of w. *Exam.* ཡི་དྭགས་ ye-daw.

SECTION VII.

The Tibetians have at the end of their Alphabet a series of letters which they use to write Sanskrit words, they are the following:

ཊ་	ཋ་	ཌྷ་	ཌ་	ཎ་	ཥ་	གྷ་	དྷ་	བྷ་	ཛྙ་	ཀྵ་
ta	tha	dha	da	na	sha	gha	dha	bha	gna	khya

Observations.

ཊ་ ta, the English t; the Bengalee ট.

ཋ་ tha, the English t, aspirated; the Bengalee ঠ.

ཌ་ dha, as the English d; the Bengalee ড.

ཌྷ་ dha, as the English d, aspirated; the Bengalee ঢ

ཎ་ na, as the English n, or Bengalee ণ.

ཥ་ sha, is also pronounced kha; the Bengalee ষ.

གྷ་ gha, as the English g, in give; or Bengalee ঘ.

དྷ་ dha, the dental d, aspirated; the Bengalee ধ.

བྷ་ bha, as the English b, aspirated; the Bengalee ভ.

ཛྙ་ gn*i*ya, a nasal sound, corresponding with the Bengalee জ্ঞ.

ཀྵ་ khya, corresponding with the Bengalee ক্ষ.

The subsequent is a table which exhibits all the superscribed mute letters, mentioned in the preceding rules.

ཀླ་	གླ་	བླ་	ཟླ་	རླ་	སླ་	ལྐ་	ལྒ་	ལྔ་	ལྕ་
la	la	la	da	la	la	ka	ga	nga	cha

རྗ་	རྟ་	རྡ་	ལྤ་	རྦ་	སྡ་	སྟ་	སྡ་	སྨྲ་	སྣྲ་
ja	ta	da	pa	ba or wa	da	ta	da	mra	nra
ལྷ་	སྐ་	སྒ་	སྔ་	སྙ་	སྐྱ་	སྒྱ་	སྤྱ་	ཕྱ་	སྦྱ་
lha	ka	ga	nga	nya	k'ya	g'ya	cha	ch'ha	ja
སྟ་	སྡ་	སྣ་	སྤ་	སྥ་	སྨྱ་	རྒྱ་	ལྒྱ་		
ta	da	na	pa	p'ha	nya	gya	g'ya		
སྦ་	སྨ་	སྩ་	རྫ་	སྟ་					
ba	ma	tsa	dsa	ta					

Though one sound may be expressed in so many different ways, yet in writing and reading, the greatest attention ought to be paid to them, as the meaning of the thing expressed depends on the mute letter which is used, for instance, ལྔ nga, signifies *five*, but རྔ nga, signifies, *a drum*.

SECTION VIII.

Having found the translating the English Alphabet into Tibetian, and placing all the letters and syllables of one sound in one row, to be useful in studying the alphabet, I will here do the same to assist the learner to read Tibetian without having occasion to consult the rules, which have been laid down.

The Tibetian characters and syllables corresponding with them.

	English letters.	*Nagree corresponding letters.*
	a, འ་ ཨ་ ཨོཾ་ or ཨཀཱལ།	अ आ
	b, འབ་ འབའ་ སྦ་ བོ་ སྦྲ་།	ब
	ch, as in church, ཅ་ ལྕ་ པཙའ་ ཀཙའ་ སྤྱ་ སྤྱུ་ སྤྱ་།	च
Aspirated	chh, ཆ་ ཕྱ་ ཁྱ་ ཕྱ་ འཆའ་ མཆའ་།	छ
English	d, ཕག་ མག་ དག་ པག་ སྦ་ སྒྲ་ འད་ འན་།	ड
English	dh, ག་ ད་ ན་ ཏ་།	ढ

English letters.		*Nagree corresponding letters.*
Dental	d, གདའ་ མདའ་ བདའ་ར་ལྡ་སྡ་ཟླ་།	द
Dental	dh, ད་།	ध
	e, འེ་ ཨེ་།	ए
	g, དགའ་ འགའ་ མགའ་ རྒ་ ལྒ་ སྒ་ བསྒ་།	ग
Aspirated	gh, ག་།	घ
	h, ཧ་།	ह
	i, འི་ ཨི་།	इ
	j, འཇ་ མཇ་ འབྱ་རྗ་ ལྗ།	ज
Aspirated	jh, ཇ་ བྱ་།	झ
	k, ཀ་ རྐ་ སྐ་ དཀའ་ བཀའ།	क
Aspirated	kh, ཁ་ འཁའ་ མཁའ།	ख
	l, ལ་ སླ་ ཟླ་ རླ་ ཀླ་ བླ།	ल
	m, མ་རྨ་སྨ་དམའ།	म
	n, ན་རྣ་སྣ་མནའ།	न
	o, འོ་ ཨོ་།	ओ
	p, པ་སྤ་ལྤ་དཔར།	प
Aspirated	ph, ཕ་འཕའ།	फ
	r, ར།	र
	s, ས་ བཟའ་ བསའ་ གསའ།	स
	sh, ཤ་ གཤའ་ བཤའ་།	श
English	t, ཊ་ ཏ་ སྟ སྟ ཊ།	ट
English	th, ཋ ཐ ཐ ཋ།	ठ
Dental	t, ཏ་ རྟ་ ལྟ་ སྟ་ གཏའ་ བཏའ།	त
Dental	th, ཐ་ སྠ་ མཐའ་ འཐ།	थ
	u, འུ་ཨུ་དབུ་།	उ
	w, དབའ་ ཝ།	व
	y, ཡ་དབྱ་གཡའ།	य

For letters not corresponding with these in the English Alphabet, see the Alphabet.

SECTION IX.

Of Numerals.

The Cardinal Numbers, from one to one hundred, with the European and Tibet figures adopted to represent them, are as follows:

Figures.				
European.	*Tibet.*		*Denomination.*	
1	༡	གཅིག་	chigh.	
2	༢	གཉིས་	nyi.	
3	༣	གསུམ་	soom.	
4	༤	བཞི་	shi.	
5	༥	ལྔ་	nga.	
6	༦	དྲུག་	dhoogh.	
7	༧	བདུན་	dün.	
8	༨	བརྒྱད་	gyed.	
9	༩	དགུ་	goo.	
10	༡༠	བཅུ་ ཐམས་ པ་	chootham-bha.	
11	༡༡	བཅུ་ གཅིག་	choo-chigh.	
12	༡༢	བཅུ་ གཉིས་	choo nyi.	
13	༡༣	བཅུ་ གསུམ་	choo soom.	
14	༡༤	བཅུ་ བཞི་	choo shi.	
15	༡༥	བཅུ་ ལྔ་	choo nga.	
16	༡༦	བཅུ་ དྲུག་	choo dhoog.	
17	༡༧	བཅུ་ བདུན་	choo dün	
18	༡༨	བཅུ་ བརྒྱད་	choo g'yed.	
19	༡༩	བཅུ་ དགུ་	choo goo.	
20	༢༠	ཉི་ ཤུ་	nyi shoo.	ཉི་ ཤུ་ ཐམ་པ།
21	༢༡	ཉེར་ གཅིག་	nyer chigh.	ཉེ་ གཅིག་ །
22	༢༢	ཉེར་ གཉིས་	nyer, n'yi.	ཉེ་ གཉིས་ །
23	༢༣	ཉེར་ གསུམ་	nyer soom.	

Figures.				
European.	*Tibet.*		*Denomination.*	
24	༢༤	ཉེར་བཞི་	nyer shi.	
25	༢༥	ཉེར་ལྔ་	nyer nga.	
26	༢༦	ཉེར་དྲུག་	nyer dhoogh.	
27	༢༧	ཉེར་བདུན་	nyer dün.	
28	༢༨	ཉེར་བརྒྱད་	nyer gyed.	
29	༢༩	ཉེར་དགུ་	nyer goo.	
30	༣༠	སུམ་ཅུ་ .	soom choo.	སུམ་ཅུ་ཐམས་པ་
31	༣༡	སོ་གཅིག་	so chigh.	
32	༣༢	སོ་གཉིས་	so nyi.	
33	༣༣	སོ་གསུམ་	so soom.	
34	༣༤	སོ་བཞི་	so shi.	
35	༣༥	སོ་ལྔ་	so nga.	
36	༣༦	སོ་དྲུག་	so dhoogh.	
37	༣༧	སོ་བདུན་	so dün.	
38	༣༨	ས་བརྒྱད་	so gyed.	
39	༣༩	སོ་དགུ་	so goo.	
40	༤༠	བཞི་བཅུ་	shi choo.	བཞི་བཅུ་ཐམས་པ
41	༤༡	ཞེ་གཅིག་	she chigh.	
42	༤༢	ཞེ་གཉིས་	she nyi.	
43	༤༣	ཞེ་གསུམ་	she soom.	
44	༤༤	ཞེ་བཞི་	she shi.	
45	༤༥	ཞེ་ལྔ་	she nga.	
46	༤༦	ཞེ་དྲུག་	she dhoogh.	
47	༤༧	ཞེ་བདུན་	she dün.	
48	༤༨	ཞེ་བརྒྱད་	she gyed.	
49	༤༩	ཞེ་དགུ་	she goo.	
50	༥༠	ལྔ་བཅུ་	nga choo.	
51	༥༡	ང་གཅིག་	nga chigh.	

Figures. European.	Tibet.		*Denomination.*	
52	༥༢	ང་གཉིས་	nga nyi.	
53	༥༣	ང་གསུམ་	nga soom.	
54	༥༤	ང་བཞི་	nga shi.	
55	༥༥	ང་ལྔ་	nga nga.	
56	༥༦	ང་དྲུག་	nga dhoogh.	
57	༥༧	ང་བདུན་	nga dün.	
58	༥༨	ང་བརྒྱད་	nga gye.	
59	༥༩	ང་དགུ་	nga goo.	
60	༦༠	དྲུག་ཅུ་	dhoog choo.	དྲུག་བཅུ་ཐམས་པ།
61	༦༡	རེ་གཅིག་	re chigh.	
62	༦༢	རེ་གཉིས་	re nyee.	
63	༦༣	རེ་གསུམ་	re soom.	
64	༦༤	རེ་བཞི་	re shi.	
65	༦༥	རེ་ལྔ་	re nga.	
66	༦༦	རེ་དྲུག་	re dhoogh.	
67	༦༧	རེ་བདུན་	re dün.	
68	༦༨	རེ་བརྒྱད་	re gyed.	
69	༦༩	རེ་དགུ་	re goo.	
70	༧༠	བདུན་ཅུ་	dün choo.	བདུན་བཅུ་ཐམས་པ།
71	༧༡	དོན་གཅིག་	dön chigh.	
72	༧༢	དོན་གཉིས་	dön nyi.	
73	༧༣	དོན་གསུམ་	dön soom.	
74	༧༤	དོན་བཞི་	dön shi.	
75	༧༥	དོན་ལྔ་	dön nga.	
76	༧༦	དོན་དྲུག་	dön dhoogh.	
77	༧༧	དོན་བདུན་	dön dün.	
78	༧༨	དོན་བརྒྱད་	dön gyed.	
79	༧༩	རན་དགུ་	dön goo.	

Figures. European.	Tibet.		*Denomination.*	
80	༨༠	བརྒྱད་ཅུ་	gye choo.	བརྒྱད་བཅུ་ཐམས་པ།
81	༨༡	རྒྱར་གཅིག་	gya chigh	
82	༨༢	རྒྱ་གཉིས་	gya nyi.	
83	༨༣	རྒྱ་གསུམ་	gya soom.	
84	༨༤	རྒྱ་བཞི་	gya shi.	
85	༨༥	རྒྱ་ལྔ་	gya nga.	
86	༨༦	རྒྱ་དྲུག་	gya dhoogh.	
87	༨༧	རྒྱ་བདུན་	gya dün.	
88	༨༨	རྒྱ་བརྒྱད་	gya gyed	
89	༨༩	རྒྱ་དགུ་	gya goo.	
90	༩༠	དགུ་བཅུ་	goo choo.	དགུ་བཅུ་ཐམས་པ།
91	༩༡	གོ་གཅིག་	go chigh.	
92	༩༢	གོ་གཉིས་	go nyi.	
93	༩༣	གོ་གསུམ་	go soom.	
94	༩༤	གོ་བཞི་	go shi.	
95	༩༥	གོ་ལྔ་	go nga.	
96	༩༦	གོ་དྲུག་	go dhoogh.	
97	༩༧	གོ་བདུན་	go dün.	
98	༩༨	གོ་བརྒྱད་	go gyed.	
99	༩༩	གོ་དགུ་	go goo.	
100	༡༠༠	བརྒྱ་ཐམ་པ་	gya tham pa.	བརྒྱ་ཐམས་པ།
101	༡༠༡	བརྒྱ་གཅིག་	gya chigh.	
102	༡༠༢	བརྒྱ་གཉིས་	gya nyi.	
103	༡༠༣	བརྒྱ་གསུམ་	gya soom.	
110	༡༡༠	བརྒྱ་བཅུ་	gya choo.	
115	༡༡༥	བརྒྱ་བཅུ་ལྔ་	gya choo nga.	
200	༢༠༠	ཉིས་བརྒྱ་	nyee gya.	
1000	༡༠༠༠	སྟོང་ཕྲག་	dong-dhagh.	

SECTION X.

Abbreviations, (འདུས་ཡིག་ན།)

The following are often used in writing.

ཐཾད་	*for*	ཐམས་ཅད་	thamche ; *all.*
ཕྱོན་	......	ཕྱོགས་	chho ; *country, quarter, part.*
ལྕྒ་	......	ལྕགས་	cha ; *iron.*
བཅྀག་	......	བཅུ་གཅིག་	choo chigh ; *eleven.*
བཅིཉ་	......	བཅུ་གཉིས།	choo nyi ; *twelve.*
ཉིུ་	......	ཉི་ཤུ་	nyi shoo ; *twenty.*
འཁོཪ་	......	འཁོར་ལོ།	khorlo ; *a wheel.*
མནྨསོ་	......	མ་ན་མ་སོ་	manamasi ; *birth.*
རྗེ་	......	རྡོ་རྗེ་	dor-je ; *the club in Indra's hand.*
བཅོཾ་	......	བཅོམ་ལྡན་འདས་	chomdende ; *Boodh.*
ཡོནྟ་མ་	......	ཡོན་ཏན་མ་	yön-ten-ma ; *goddess Ooma.*
རྗེ་འི་མཆུ་	......	རྡོ་རྗེའི་མཆུ་	dojei chhoo ; G*u*nesh*a*, the son of Sh*i*v*a* and Ooma.
ཕྱལྡན་	......	འཕྱག་འཚལ་ལྡན།	chhagh-tshal-den ; *Indra.*
རྒྱལོའི་རྒྱལོ་	......	རྒྱལ་པོའི་རྒྱལ་པོ།	gyal-poi gyalpo ; *King of kings.*
སངྒྱས་	......	སངས་རྒྱས།	sang-gye ; *Boodh.*
སེཾའ་ཆེ་	......	སེམས་དཔའ་ཆེ།	sem-pa-chhe ; *very wise or learned.*
མགྲོའི་དབྱུག་	......	མཁའ་འགྲོའི་དབང་ཕྱུག་	khadoiwangchhoo ; *the bird Guroora in Paradise.*
སེཾགྒེའི་ཤིངྟ་	......	སེང་གེའི་ཤིང་རྟ།	seng-ghei shing-ta ; *riding upon a lion.*
དུཀྱི་དགའམ་	......	དུས་ཀྱི་དགའ་མ།	dhü-kyi gama ; *name of Ooma.*
སེཾན་	......	སེམས་ཅན།	sem-chen ; *creature, animal.*
ཡོནྟ་	......	ཡོན་ཏན།	yon-ten ; *virtue, ability.*
སོཾར་	......	སོ་སོར།	so-sor ; *various.*

PART II.

Of the Parts of Speech.

There are eight Parts of Speech: Noun Substantive, Adjective, Pronoun, Verb, Adverb, Preposition, Conjunction, and Interjection.

The Particle ནི་ answers to the article 'the' for instance, མིད་པས་ནི, *the throat;* བྱེད་ཟག་ནི་ *the business, work.*

SECTION I.

Of the Noun Substantive.

A word which can be declined through different numbers and cases, is called a Noun; of which we have to observe,

1st. The *Gender*, or distinction of sex, whether Masculine, Feminine, or Neuter.

2d. The *Number*, i. e. the Singular or Plural.

3d. The *Case*, or the different terminations or endings of a noun; these are:

The Nominative; the Genitive; the Dative; the Accusative; the Vocative, and the Ablative.

4th. The *Declension* which is produced by the various Cases and Numbers.

Of the Gender.

Masculine Nouns end in པོ་; Feminine Nouns in མོ་; for instance, མགྲོན་པོ། *a host.* མགྲོན་མོ། *an hostess.*

In masculine and feminine nouns, the different cases are formed by affixing the following terminations:

Genitive.	ཀྱི་ཀྱི་ འི་ཡི་	Ablative.	ནས་ལས་
Dative.	ལ་	Instrumental.	ར་
Accusative.	ལུ་	Locative.	ར་ལས་སུ་ཏུ་དུ་ན་ར་

Remarks on the Sign of the Genitive.

If the word end in ད་བ་ས་ the possessive case must be formed by ཀྱི ; *Exam.* ཁྱེད་ཀྱི་, your, རྒྱབ་ཀྱི་, of a side, གཡས་ཀྱི་, of the right.

If the word terminate in ག་ང་ the genitive or possessive case must end in གི་ ; *Exam.* བདག་གི །, mine ; རྐང་གི་, of the foot.

If the word terminate in a vowel the genitive is to be expressed by འི་ or ཡི་ ; *Exam.* མའི་, of a mother ; སའི་, of earth ; ཆུའི་, of water ; ཉིའི་, of a day.

If the word terminate in ན་མ་ར་ལ་, the possessive or genitive case must be expressed by གྱི་ ; *Exam.* དོན་གྱི་, of a cause ; ཤར་གྱི་, of the east ; གཏམ་གྱི་, of a word ; དཔལ་གྱི་, of riches, grandeur, or excellency.

The same rules are applicable to the instrumental, གྱིས་ ཀྱིས་ གྱིས་ གྲི་ཨེ་, with the knife ; here is ཨེ་ e, the sign of the instrumental.

Remarks on the Sign of the Locative.

If the word terminate in ག་ བ་, the locative case must be expressed by ཏུ་ ; *Exam.* ཐག་ ཏུ་, རབ་ ཏུ་ །

If the word terminate in ང་ ད་ ན་ མ་ ར་ ལ་ the locative case must be expressed by དུ་ ; *Exam.* འབྲུང་དུ་ སྣོད་དུ་ །, in a vessel ; རྒྱུན་དུ་ ཉིམ་དུ་ མྱུར་དུ་ །, in haste.

ས་ is sometimes employed as the termination of the nominative plural.

Examples.

Singular.	*Plural.*
གློ་བ་, lungs.	གློ་བས་, lungs.
རྒྱུ་མ་, bowels.	རྒྱུ་མས་, bowels.

Observing these rules there is but one declension of nouns; nor except as above mentioned, is there any termination to express the plural number, but the plural is formed by adding the adjectives རྣམས་, ཐམས་ཅད་, all, to the singular, placing the signs of the cases after the adjectives, as will appear from the following example of a declined Noun.

Example.

	Singular.	*Plural.*
N.	ཁྱིམ་, a house.	ཁྱིམ་རྣམས་, or ཐམས་ཅད་, houses.
G.	ཁྱིམ་གྱི་, of a house.	ཁྱིམ་རྣམས་ཀྱི་, of houses.
D.	ཁྱིམ་ལ་, to a house.	ཁྱིམ་རྣམས་ལ་, to houses.
Acc.	ཁྱིམ་, a house.	ཁྱིམ་རྣམས་, houses.
Abl.	ཁྱིམ་ནས་ or ལས་, from a house.	ཁྱིམ་རྣམས་ནས་, or ལས་, from houses.
Inst.	ཁྱིམ་གྱིས་ or ཁྱིམས་, with or by a house.	ཁྱིམ་རྣམས་ཀྱིས་, with or by houses.
Loc.	ཁྱིམ་དུ་ or ན་ or ལ་, in a house.	ཁྱིམ་རྣམས་སུ, in houses.

	Singular.	*Plural.*
N.	མ་, a mother.	མ་ཐམས་ཅད་, mothers.
G.	མའི་, a mother's.	མ་ཐམས་ཅད་ཀྱི་, mothers'.
D.	མལ་, to a mother.	མ་ཐམས་ཅད་ལ་, to mothers.
Acc.	མ་ལ་, a mother.	མ་ཐམས་ཅད་ལ་, mothers.
Abl.	མ་ནས་ or ལས་, from a mother.	མ་ཐམས་ཅད་ལས་ or ནས་, from mothers.
Inst.	མ་གྱིས་, by a mother.	མ་ཐམས་ཅད་ཀྱིས་, with or by mothers.
Loc.	མ་ལ་, in a mother.	མ་ཐམས་ཅད་དུ, or ན or ལ་, in mothers.

The word ཚོགས་ signifying many, a multitude, may also be employed to form the plural number;

Example.

	Singular.	*Plural.*
N.	ཡབ་ a father.	ཡབ་ཚོགས་, fathers.
G.	ཡབ་ཀྱི, a father's.	ཡབ་ཚོགས་ཀྱི་, fathers'.
D.	ཡབ་ལ, to a father.	ཡབ་ཚོགས་ལ་, to fathers.
Acc.	ཡབ་ལ་, a father.	ཡབ་ཚོགས་ལ་, fathers.

	Singular	*Plural.*
Abl.	ཡབ་ནས or ལས་, from a father.	ཡབ་ཚོགས་ལས་ or ནས་, from fathers.
Inst.	ཡབས་ཡབ་ཀྱིས་, by or with a father.	ཡབ་ཚོགས་ཀྱིས་, by or with fathers.
Loc.	ཡབ་དུ་, in a father.	ཡབ་ཚོགས་སུ, in fathers.

N.	ཆུ་, water.	Abl.	ཆུ་ནས་, from water.
G.	ཆུའི་, of water.	Inst.	ཆུར་ or ཆུས་, by water.
D.	ཆུ་ལ་, to water.	Loc.	ཆུ་ལ་ or ཆུ་རུ་ or ཆུ་ན་ or ཆུ་སུ, in water.
Acc.	ཆུ་ལ, water.		

SECTION II.

Of Nouns Adjective.

An Adjective expresses the quality of a thing. It may be declined like a noun substantive, and then receives the same signs of the cases. When placed after a noun substantive; it stands thus, ཤིང་ a tree, and མང་པོ་ many, written ཤིང་མང་པོ་ and declined in the following manner.

Example.

N.	ཤིང་མང་པོ་ ། many trees.	Abl.	ཤིང་མང་པོ་ནས or ལས་ ། from many trees.
G.	ཤིང་མང་པོའི་ of many trees.		
D.	ཤིང་མང་པ་ལ་ ། to many trees.	Inst.	ཤིང་མང་པོས་, by many trees.
Acc.	ཤིང་མང་པོ་ལ ། many trees.	Loc.	ཤིང་མབ་པོ་ན་ or དུ་, in or among many trees.

	Singular.	*Plural.*
N.	གཟུགས་མཛེས་, a fine body.	གཟུགས་མཛེས་རྣམས་ ། fine bodies.
G.	གཟུགས་མཛེས་ཀྱི།, of a fine body.	གཟུགས་མཛེས་རྣམས་ཀྱི།, of fine bodies.
D.	གཟུགས་མཛེས་ལ ། to a fine body.	གཟུགས་མཛེས་རྣམས་ལ་ ། to fine bodies.
Acc.	གཟུགས་མཛེས་ལ ། a fine body.	གཟུགས་མཛེས་རྣམས་ལ་ ། fine bodies.
Abl.	གཟུགས་མཛེས་ནས་ or ལས་, from a fine body.	གཟུགས་མཛེས་རྣམས་ལས་ or ནས་, from fine bodies.
Inst.	གཟུགས་མཛེས་ཀྱིས་, by or with a fine body.	གཟུགས་མཛེས་རྣམས་ཀྱིས, by or with fine bodies.
Loc.	གཟུགས་མཛེས་དུ་ or སུ་, in a fine body.	གཟུགས་མཛེས་རྣམས་དུ་ or ན་ or ལ་, or ས་, in fine bodies.

Of the Comparison of Adjectives.

There are three degrees of comparison, the positive, the comparative, and the superlative.

The comparative is formed by affixing བས་ or ལས་ to the positive; and the superlative is formed by prefixing རབ་ཏུ་ or ཤིན་ཏུ་ before the positive; for instance, the adjective in the positive, ཆེན་པོ་ great, will be in the comparative ཆེན་པོ་བས་ or ཆེན་པོ་ལས་ greater, and in the superlative རབ་ཏུ་ཆེན་པོ་ or ཤིན་ཏུ་ཆེན་པོ་ very great or greatest. *Exam.* མེ་བས་ཚ་ hotter than fire.

SECTION III.

Of Pronouns.

Pronouns are declined like Nouns, as follows; thus; ང་ I;.

	Singular.	*Plural.*
N.	ང་, I.	ང་རྣམས་, we,
G.	ང་འི་ or ངཡི་ or ངཡིས་, mine, or my.	ང་རྣམས་ཀྱི, our, our's.
D.	ང་ལ་, to me.	ང་རྣམས་ལ་, to us.
Acc.	ང་ལ་, me.	ང་རྣམས་ལ་, us.
Abl.	ང་ནས་ or ལས་, from me.	ང་རྣམས་ནས་ or ལས་, from us.
Inst.	ངར་ or ངས་ or ང་ ཀྱིས་, by or with me.	ང་རྣམས་ཀྱིས་, with or by us.
Loc.	ང་ན་ or ང་ཏུ་ or ང་ར་ང་ལ་ or ང་སུ་, in me.	ང་རྣམས་ན་ or ཏུ་ or སུ་ or ལ་, in us.

	Singular.	*Plural.*
N.	ངེད་, I.	ངེད་རྣམས་, we.
G.	ངེད་ཀྱི་, mine, my.	ངེད་རྣམས་ཀྱི་, our, our's.
D.	ངེད་ལ་, to me.	ངེད་རྣམས་ལ་, to us.
Acc.	ངེད་ལ་, me.	ངེད་རྣམས་ལ་, us.
Abl.	ངེད་ནས་ or ལས་, from me.	ངེད་རྣམས་ལས་ or ནས་, from us.
Inst.	ངེད་ཀྱིས་, with or by me.	ངེད་རྣམ ས་ཀྱིས་, with or by us.
Loc.	ངེད་ན་ལ་ or ར་, in me.	ངེད་རྣམས་ན་ or སུ་ or ཏུ་, in us.

	Singular.	*Plural.*
N.	ཁྱེད་ or ཁྱོད, thou.	ཁྱོད་ཐམས་ཅད་, you.
G.	ཁྱེད་ཀྱི་ or ཁྱོད་ཀྱི་, thine, thy.	ཁྱོད་ཐམས་ཅད་ཀྱི་, your, your's.
D.	ཁྱེད་ལ་ or ཁྱོད་ལ་, to thee.	ཁྱོད་ཐམས་ཅད་ལ་, to you.
Acc.	ཁྱེད་ལ་ or ཁྱོད་ལ་, thee.	ཁྱོད་ཐམས་ཅད་ལ་, you.
Abl.	ཁྱེད་ནས་ or ཁྱོད་ནས་ or ལས་. from thee.	ཁྱོད་ཐམས་ཅད་ནས་ or ལས་, from you.
Inst.	ཁྱེད་ཀྱིས་ or ཁྱོད་ཀྱིས་, with or by thee.	ཁྱོད་ཐམས་ཅད་ཀྱིས་, with or by you.
Loc.	ཁྱེད་ན or ཁྱོད་ན་ or རུ་ or ལ་, in thee.	ཁྱོད་ཐམས་ཅད་ན་ or རུ་, in you.

The following word is used when the person or thing spoken of is at a distance.

He, or she.

	Singular.	*Plural.*
N.	ཕ་གི་, he, she.	ཕ་གི་ཚོགས་ །, they, those.
G.	ཕ་གིའི་, his, her's.	ཕ་གི་ཚོགས་ཀྱི་ or ཕ་གི་ཚོའི །, their, their's.
D.	ཕ་གི་ལ་, to him, to her.	ཕ་གི་ཚོགས་ལ, to them.
Acc.	ཕ་གི་ལ་, him, her.	ཕ་གི་ཚོགས་ལ་, them.
Abl.	ཕ་གི་ནས་ or ལས, from him, from her.	ཕ་གི་ཚོགས་ནས་ or ལས་, from them.
Inst.	ཕ་གིས་, by him, by her.	ཕ་གི་ཚོགས་ཀྱིས་, by them.
Loc.	ཕ་གི་ན་, in him, in her.	ཕ་གི་ཚོགས་ན་, or རུ, in them.

When the person or thing spoken of is near.

He, she.

	Singular.	*Plural.*
N.	ཁང་, he, she.	ཁོང་རྣམས་, they, these.
G.	ཁོང་གི་, his, her's.	ཁོང་རྣམས་ཀྱི །, of these.
D.	ཁོང་ལ, to him to her.	ཁོང་རྣམས་ལ །, to these.
Acc.	ཁོང་ལ་, him, her.	ཁོང་རྣམས་ལ །, these.
Abl.	ཁང་ནས or ལས་, from him, from her.	ཁོང་རྣམས་ནས་ or ལས་, from these.
Inst.	ཁོང་གིས་, with or by him, or her.	ཁོང་རྣམས་ཀྱིས་, with or by these.
Loc.	ཁོང་ན་ or རུ, in him, or her.	ཁོང་རྣམས་ན or རུ or སུ, in these.

	Singular.	*Plural.*
N.	ངེད་ཉིད་ or ང་རང་, I myself.	ངེད་རྣམས་ཉིད་, we ourselves.
G.	ངེད་ཉིད་ཀྱི or ང་རང་ གི་, of myself	ངེད་རྣམས་ཉིད་ཀྱི་།, of ourselves.
D.	ངེད་ཉིད་ལ or ང་རང་ལ་, to myself.	ངེད་རྣམས་ཉིད་ལ་, to ourselves.
Acc.	ངེད་ཉིད་ལ or ང་རང་ ལ, myself.	ངེད་རྣམས་ཉིད་ལ་, ourselves.
Abl.	ངེད་ཉིད་ནས་ or ལས་ or ང་རང་ ལས་, from myself.	ངེད་རྣམས་ ཉིད་ནས་ or ལས་, from ourselves.
Inst.	ངེད་ཉིད་ཀྱིས་ or ང་རང་གིས་, by or with myself.	ངེད་རྣམས་ཉིད་ཀྱིས་, with or by ourselves.
Loc.	ངེད་ཉིད་ན or ར་ or ང་རང་ར་, in myself.	ངེད་རྣམས་ ཉིད་ན་ or ར་, in ourselves.

	Singular.	*Plural.*
N.	ཁྱེད་ཉིད་, thyself.	ཁྱེད་རྣམས་ཉིད་, yourselves.
G.	ཁྱེད་ཉིད་ཀྱི་, of thyself.	ཁྱེད་རྣམས་ཉིད་ཀྱི་, of yourselves.
D.	ཁྱེད་ཉིད་ལ་, to thyself.	ཁྱེད་རྣམས་ཉིད་ལ་།, to yourselves.
Acc.	ཁྱེད་ཉིད་ལ་, thyself.	ཁྱེད་རྣམས་ཉིད་ལ་།, yourselves.
Abl.	ཁྱེད་ཉིད་ནས་ or ལས་, from thyself.	ཁྱེད་རྣམས་ཉིད་ནས་ or ལས་, from yourselves.
Inst.	ཁྱེད་ཉིད་ཀྱིས་, with or by thyself.	ཁྱེད་རྣམས་ཉིད་ཀྱིས་, by or with yourselves.
Loc.	ཁྱེད་ཉིད་ར་, in thyself.	ཁྱེད་རྣམས་ཉིད་ར་, in yourselves.

	Singular.	*Plural.*
N.	ཁྱོད་རང་, thyself.	ཁྱོད་རྣམས་རང་, yourselves.
G.	ཁྱོད་རང་གི་, of thyself.	ཁྱེད་རྣམས་རང་གི་, of yourselves.
D.	ཁྱོད་རང་ལ་, to thyself.	ཁྱོད་རྣམས་རང་ལ་, to yourselves.
Acc.	ཁྱོད་རང་ལ་, thyself.	ཁྱོད་རྣམས་རང་ལ་, yourselves.
Abl.	ཁྱོད་རང་ནས་ or ལས་, from thyself.	ཁྱོད་རྣམས་རང་ནས་ or ལས་, from yourselves
Inst.	ཁྱོད་རང་གིས་, with or by thyself.	ཁྱོད་རྣམས་རང་གིས, by or with yourselves.
Loc.	ཁྱོད་རང་ར་, in thyself.	ཁྱོད་རྣམས་རང་ར་, in yourselves.

	Singular.	*Plural.*
N.	ཁོ་རང་, he himself.	ཁོང་རྣམས་རང་།, they themselves.
G.	ཁོ་རང་གི་, of himself.	ཁོང་རྣམས་རང་གི་, of themselves.
D.	ཁོ་རང་ལ, to himself.	ཁོང་རྣམས་རང་ལ, to themselves.
Acc.	ཁོ་རང་ལ་, himself.	ཁོང་རྣམས་རང་ལ་, themselves.

	Singular.	*Plural.*
Abl.	ཁོ་རང་ནས་ or ལས་, from himself.	ཁོང་རྣམས་རང་ནས or ལས་, from themselves.
Inst.	ཁོ་རང་གིས་, by or with himself.	ཁོང་རྣམས་རང་གིས་, by or with themselves.
Loc.	ཁ་རང་རུ་, in himself.	ཁོང་རྣམས་རང་རུ་, in themselves.

	Singular.	*Plural.*
N,	འདི་, this.	འདི་རྣམས་ or འདི་ཚོགས་, these.
G.	འདིའི་, of this.	འདི་རྣམག་གྱི་ or འདི་ཚོའི་, of these.
D.	འདིལ་, to this.	འདི་རྣམས་ལ་ or འདི་ཚོ་ལ་, to these.
Acc.	འདིལ་, this.	འདི་རྣམས་ལ་ or འདི་ཚོ་ལ་, these.
Abl.	འདི་ནས or ལས་, from this.	འདི་རྣམས་ནས་ or ལས་, from these.
Inst.	འདི་ཀྱིས་, by this, with this.	འདི་རྣམས་ཀྱིས་, with or by these.
Loc.	འདི་ན་ or འདི་ལ།, in this.	འདི་རྣམས་ན or རུ or སུ་, in these.

Singular.

N.	དེ་, it, that.	Abl.	དེ་ནས or ལས་, from it, from that.
G.	དེའི་, of it, of that.	Inst.	དེ་གིས་, by it, by that.
D.	དེ་ལ་, to it, to that.	Loc.	དེ་ན་, in it, in that.
Acc.	དེ་ལ་, it, that.		

Of the Interrogative.

Singular.

N.	ཅ་, who? which? what?	Abl.	ཅི་ནས་ or ལས་, from whom? from what?
G.	ཅིའི་, whose? of what?	Inst.	ཅི་ཀྱིས་, by whom? by what?
D.	ཅི་ལ་, to whom? to what?	Loc.	ཅི་ན་ or རུ or སུ or ལ་, in whom? in what?
Acc.	ཅིལ་, whom? what?		

Singular.

N.	སུ་, who? which? what?	Abl.	སུ་ནས or སུ་ལས་, from whom?
G.	སུའི་, whose?	Inst.	སུ་ཀྱིས་རང་, by whom? with whom
D.	སུ་ལ་, for whom?	Loc.	སུ་ལ་ or ན་ or རུ, སུ་སུ་, in whom?
Acc.	སུ་ལ་, whom?		

Singular and Plural.

N.	གང་, what?	Abl.	གང་ནས་ or ལས་ from what?
G.	གང་གི་, of what?	Inst.	གང་གིས་ or གང་གྱིས་, with or by what?
D.	གང་ལ་, to what?	Loc.	གང་རུ་ གང་ན་ གང་ལ་ གང་སུ་, in what?
Acc.	གང་ལ་, what?		

The Thibetians besides this Interrogative Pronoun, employ the syllable འམ am, affixed to the end of the question, as an Interrogative sign. It may be affixed to the following nine letters ག་ང་ན་བ་མ་ར་ལ་ས་འ་; the last consonant of the syllable, or the final letter must be repeated. *Exam.* འཛག་གམ། ཡོད་དམ། ཡིན་ནམ། ཁྱབ་བམ། ཐམས་མམ། འགྱུར་རམ། འཚོལ་ལམ། ཤེལ་སོ་གོ་འོ་ །ཀའོ་ །

Indefinites.

N.	ལ་ལ་ཉི་ །, a, any, some.	Abl.	ལ་ལ་ནས་ or ལ་ལ་ལ་ས །, from any, from some.
G.	ལ་ལ་འི་ །, of any, of some.	Inst.	ལ་ལ་ཞས་ or ལ་ལས་ །, with any, with some.
D.	ལ་ལ་ལ་ །, to any, to some.	Loc,	ལ་ལ་ལ་ or ལ་ལ་རུ, in any, in some.
Acc.	ལ་ལ་ལ་ །, any, some.		

SECTION IV.

Of Verbs.

1st. A Verb is a word which signifies to do, or to be, and which is conjugated through certain modes, times, persons, and numbers.

2d. The Thebetians have in their language but one conjugation.

3d. There are two voices, the active which signifies to do, and the passive which signifies to be.

4th. There are three modes the indicative, the subjunctive and the imperative.

5th. There are six tenses or times, the present, the imperfect, the perfect, the pluperfect, the future imperfect (shall or will) and the future perfect (shall or will have.)

6th. As in the declensions of nouns substantive, so in the conjugation of verbs there is no distinction between the singular and the plural number.

7th. The Imperative in the second person singular, being the most simple form of the verb, may be considered as the root from which all other tenses are formed. *Exam.* བྱེད་ make, do ; སོང་ go. ཁྱེར bring.

8th. The Infinitive is made by adding པ་ or བ་ to the root;

Examples.

From བྱེད་, do, make, is formed བྱེད་པ་, to do, to make.
—— སོང་, go, —— སོང་བ་, to go.
—— ཁྱེར་, bring, —— ཁྱེར་བ་, to bring.

The infinitive may also be used as a noun substantive.

9th. The Present Participle is formed by adding འི་ to the Infinitive mode ; for instance,

From བྱེད་པ་, to do, is formed བྱེད་པའི་, doing.
—— སོང་བ་, to go, —— སོང་བའི, going.
—— ཁྱེར་བ་, to bring, —— ཁྱེར་བའི་, bringing.

The Conjugation of the Verb

འགྲོ་བ་ to go.

Indicative, Present.

Singular.	*Plural.*
1 ང་ འགྲོ་གི, or ངས་འགྲོ་གི །, or འགྲོ་བ་ཡིན །, I go.	ངེད་ or ངེད་རྣམས་ or ངར་རྣམས་ཀྱིས་འགྲོ་གི, we go.
2 ཁྱེད་, or ཁྱོད་རང་, or ཁྱེད་རང་འགྲོ་གི །, thou goest.	ཁྱེད་རྣམས་ འགྲོ་ གི །, ye go.
3 ཁ་རང་ འགྲོ་གི །, he goes.	ཁོ་རང་རྣམས་འགྲོ་གི་ །, they go.

Imperfect.

Singular.

1. ང་ འགྲོ་བ་ཡིན་ །, I went.
2. ཁྱེ་རང་ འགྲོ་བ་ཡིན །, thou wentest.
3. ཁོ་རང་ འགྲོ་བ་ཡིན་, he went.

Plural.

1. ངེད་རྣམས་ འགྲོ་བ་ཡིན་།, we went.
2. ཁྱེད་རྣམས་ འགྲོ་བ་ཡིན་ །. ye went.
3. ཁོ་རང་རྣམས་ འགྲོ་བ་ཡིན །, they went.

Perfect Definite.

Singular.

1. ང་ འགྲོ་སོང་བ་ །, I have gone.
2. ཁྱེད་ འགྲོ་སོང་བ།, thou hast gone.
3. ཁོ་རང་ འགྲོ་སོང་བ་ །, he has gone.

Plural.

1. ངེད་རྣམས་ འགྲོ་སོང་བ།, we have gone.
2. ཁྱེད་རྣམས་ འགྲོ་སོང་བ །, ye have gone.
3. ཁོ་རང་རྣམས་ འགྲོ་སོང་བ །, they have gone.

Perfect Indefinite.

Singular.

1. ང་ འགྲོ་སོང་ །, I went.
2. ཁྱེད་ འགྲོ་སོང །, thou wentest.
3. ཁོ་རང་ འགྲོ་སོང, he went.

Plural.

1. ངེད་རྣམས་ འགྲོ་སོང །, we went
2. ཁྱེད་རྣམས་ འགྲོ་སོང །. ye went.
3. ཁོ་རང་རྣམས་ འགྲོ་སོང །, they went.

Pluperfect.

Singular.

1. ང་ འགྲོ་སོང་བ་ཡིན་ །, I had gone.
2. ཁྱེད་ འགྲོ་སོང་བ་ཡིན་ །, thou hadst gone.
3. ཁོ་རང་ འགྲོ་སོང་བ་ཡིན་ །, he had gone.

Plural.

1. ངེད་རྣམས་ འགྲོ་སོང་བ་ཡིན་ །, we had gone.
2. ཁྱེད་རྣམས་ འགྲོ་སོང་བ་ཡིན་ །, ye had gone.
3. ཁོ་རང་རྣམས་ འགྲོ་སོང་བ་ཡིན་ །, they had gone.

Future.

Singular.

1. ང་ འགྲོ་ཀི་ཡུ །, I shall or will go.
2. ཁྱེད་ འགྲོ་ཀི་ཡུ །, thou shalt or wilt go.
3. ཁོ་རང་ འགྲོ་ཀི་ཡུ །, he shall or will go.

Plural.

1. ངེད་རྣམས་ འགྲོ་ཀི་ཡུ །, we shall or will go.
2. ཁྱེད་རྣམས་ འགྲོ་ཀི་ཡུ །, ye shall or will go.
3. ཁོ་རང་རྣམས་ འགྲོ་ཀི་ཡུ །, they shall or will go.

Imperative.

འགྲོ or འགྲོ་ཅིག །, go thou.

Infinitive.

འགྲོ་བ་ །, going, to go.

Gerund.

འགྲོ་བས། , going.

Participle.

Past. འགྲོ་ནས་། , gone, having gone.

Pres. འགྲོ་བའི་, going, or that goes.

Ger. འགྲོ་བའི་ཕྱིར། , to go.

Gerund. འགྲོ་བའི་དོན་དུ་, for the going.

Present.

Singular.	*Plural.*
1. ང་ཡིན། , I am.	ངར་རྣམས་ཡིན། , we are.
2. ཁྱོད་ཡིན། , thou art.	ཁྱོད་རྣམས་ཡིན། , ye are.
3. ཡིན་ཏེ་། ཡོད། , he is.	ཁོང་རྣམས་ཡིན། , they are.

Future.

1. ང་ཡིང། , I shall be.
2. ཁྱོད་ཡོང། , thou shall be.
3. ཁོ་མི་ཡེང། , he shall be.

***Note by the Editor.*—The past tenses of this verb, and the conjugation of a verb in the passive voice; as also the observations on indeclineable words, and the Syntax, are wanting in the author's Manuscript.**

F 2

COLLOQUIES.

ཁྱོད་ཁྲོམ་ལ་སོང་།, (khyödh thom la song,) go to the Market.

ཡང་ཙར་ངེད་ཚོའི་འཕྱིར་འབྲས་ཁྱེར་ཤོག།, (yangchar ngedhtshoi chhir de khyershogh,) and bring rice for me.

ངེད་ལྟོགས་པ་ཆེ་བར་ཡོད་།, (ngedh topa chhe bhar yödh,) I am very hungry.

དེ་ལྟའི་རྒོས་ཅི་ལྟ་ཡོད་།, (dhetai ngo chita,) what is the price of that?

རྒྱ་ཏམ་ལྔ་ངེད་ནས་ཁྱོད་ལ་སྦྱིན་ཡོངས་།, (gyetam nga nge ne khjodh la jin yong,) I will give you five rupees.

ཅི་ལྟ་ཞིག་ཁྱོད་སློངས་བ་ཡིན།, (chitashigh khyodh long wa yin,) how much do you want?

ཡང་ན་རྒྱ་ཏམ་གཅིག་སྟུད་ན་སྡིག་ཡོད་།, (yang nagya tamcheg tedh na digh yodh,) what, is not one rupee enough?

ཁོངས་གཅིག་རྒྱུ་ཆུང་ཆུང་རེད་།, (khong chigh gyoo chhoong chhoong redh,) that is a small thing.

ཡང་ཁྱོད་ངེད་ལ་རྒྱུ་ཆེ་བ་གཅིག་གཏེར་མི་ཐུབ་པམ་།, (yung khgodh nge la gyoo chhewa chig ter mi thoobh-pa ma,) what, cannot you give me a greater thing?

སྒོམ་ཁ་འབྱེ་།, (dom kha chhe,) open the trunk.

ངེད་ལྟ་རྒོས་པ་ཁྱོད་ལ་རྒྱུ་ཅི་ཡོད་།, (ngedh ta-go-pa, khyodh la gyoo chi yödh,) I will see what you have.

ཁྱོད་གཞིས་ཁ་སྦྱིན་ཡོངས་ངེ་ཡང་ན་།, (khyodh shikha jin yong nge, yang na yang,) do you pay taxes or not?

དེ་མ་སྦྱིན་ན་རྒྱལ་པོའི་ཁྱོད་ཅིངས་ཏེ་ཞག་ཡོངས་།, (dhama jin nagyah poi khyodh ching te shag yong,) If you do not pay, the raja will confine you.

ཡང་ཅར་ཁྱོད་རང་ཚོའི་ས་གཞིས་སྣངས་ཡོངས་།, (yang char khodhrangtshoi sashe langyong,) and take your ground.

འཐྲ་སྣན་།, (thaden,) take care

ཅིའི་ལབ་ཆ་ཡོད།, (chi labhchha yödh,) what do you say ?

ངེད་ ཡང་ བཤད་དགོས།, (ngedh yong shee gö,) let me also speak.

ཡིན་ནམ་མིན།, (yin nam min,) Is it, or is it not?

ས་སྟེགས་ཀྱི་འོག་ན་ ཡོད་ །, (sate kyi,) It is under the table.

ས་སྟེགས་ཀྱིས་སྟེང་ན་ཡོད ། སྟེང་ན་ཡོད་།, It is upon the table.

ཁྱོད་ངེད་ཀྱི་ཙོཀྲ་ཤོག།, come along with me.

སྔོན་ལ་སོངས།, (ngon la song,) go before.

ངེད་ཀྱི་མདུན་ལ་འགྲོ་དགོས།, (ngedh kyi dun la do gö,) come into my presence.

ནང་རུ་ཤོག།, (nang dhoo shogh,) come in.

ཕ་གི་ཚོའི་ལར་མ་འགྲོ་།, (phaghi-tshai lar ma do,) dont go among them.

འཕྱི་ལ་སོང་ །, (chhi la song,) go out.

རྗེས་ལ་འགྲོ།, (je la do,) go behind me.

ཆུའི་ཕ་རོལ་རུ་འགྲོ་།, (chhooi pharol-dhoo do,) go across the river.

དོན་མེད་ཁྱོད་སུ་ཡང་འགྲོ་མི་མེད་ཡོད་།, (dhönmedh khyödh soo yang do mi medh yong,) nobody except you is going.

ཁྱོད་དོན་ངེད་ལོང་བ་།, (khyodh dhön ngedh longwa,) I wanted it for you.

ངའི་ཁྱོད་ལ་ཅི་འཕྱིར་རྫུན་གཏམ་མི་ལབ་པ་ཡིན།, (ngai khyödh la chi chhir dsoontam milabh payin,) I am not speaking falsehoods like you.

འདི་ངོས་ཤོག།, (di ngöla shogh,) come on this side.

ཕ་གིའི་ཁ་ཐར་ངེད་ལ་ཐོབ་ཡོད།, (pha ghi-i khatar ngedh la thobh yong,) I shall get it by means of him.

དེ་བར་ངེད་ལ་མ་ཐོབ་། (dhebar ngedh la ma thobh,) I have not got it yet.

ངེད་ལབ་ཆ་དེ་ནམ་ཡང་སྨྲས་རྒྱུ་མིན།, (ngedh labh chha dhe nam yang mre gyoo min,) I shall never pronounce that word.

ནམ་ཁྱོད་ལེབ་ཡོང་ཚེ་།, (nam khyödh lebh yong tshe,) when you come back.

དེ་ནས་ངེད་འགྲོ་བའི་དང །, (dhene ngedh dowai dhang,) then I shall go.

ཞག་རེ་ཞག་རེ་ཤོག་ཡི་མ་རེ་རེ་བཞིན་ཤོག །, (share share shogh (or) ngi marereshin shogh) come daily.

ཁང་པ་ཇི་ལྟ་བུ་ཡོད་།, (khang jhitabhooyödh,) how is that?

གར་ཡོད་། ཕོ་ན་།, (ghar godh,—pho-na,) where is it! there.

ཡང་ཁོངས་འཚོའི་མི་རྣམས་ག་ན་འདུག །, (yang khong-tsho ni nam ghana doogh,) where are all those men?

ངེད་ཀྱི་དེ་མ་མཐོང་།, (ngedh kyi dhe ma thong,) I have not seen him.

དེ་ཀའི་ནན་ཏ་སོད་དང་།, (dhe koi nenta södh dhang), beat him well.

འདི་ལྟ་ཡིས། ཡང་ཁོངས་བཀའ་མི་ཉན་པར་ཡོད་འདུག །, (di- ta yi yang khong ka mi nyen par jödh doogh,) for he does not mind the order.

ངེད་ཁྱོད་ལ་ཤེས་པར་ཡོད།, (nge chhö la she par yödh,) I know you.

ཨོ་དཔོན་པོ་ཁྱོད་ཇི་ལྟར་བཀའ་བསྩལ་པ་དེ་།, (pom-po khyödh jhitar ka tsalpadhe,) O Lord, as thou hast commanded.

འདི་ལྟའི་ཁ་དོན་ལྟར་བྱས་འགྲོ་ལགས་།, (ditai kha, dhöntar jhe do la,) so it has been done.

ཁྱོད་ལཾ་ངོས་ལ་སོང་།, (khyodh lan ngö la song,) go towards the road.

ཡང་ཙར་གྲོགས་རྣམ་པ་ལ་སྨོས་ཏེ་།, (yang char dao nam la mrö ta,) and call the people.

འདི་ནི་ངོས་ཀྱི་ཁང་སོང་ཙན་།, (dine ngö kyi khyin ghang song chen) that my house may be filled.

ཡིན་ཀྱང་ངའི་ཁྱེད་ལ་ཤོད་རྒྱུ་ལ་།, (yi-kyang ngai khyedh la shodh gyoo la,) for I say unto you.

འདོད་དང་ཡང་ཙར་སྲས་སྒོ་དེ་ཆ་སྔོམ་བྱེད་དགོས་།, (dhödh dhang yang char segodhe ch-ha ngom jhedh go,) sit down and calculate the expence.

དཔལ་ལོ་ལེགྲ་བཏྲ་ཤིས་།, (pal lo le ta she,) Shree, (the goddess of prosperity), all is well. &c.

ཇི་ལྟར་ཇི་ལྟར་བཀའ་ནི་གནང་བ་ན།, (jhitar jhitar kani nang-waha,) as you command.

འདི་ལྟར་འདི་ལྟར་ངེད་ཀྱི་བྲིས་ལགས་སོ། (ditar ditar nge kyi dhe la so,) so will I write.

ངེད་ལ་ཅི་དཔོངས་པ། (nge la chi ghang yongwa,) what shall I have?

ཁྱོད་ལ་བརྙེད་པ་རབ་ཏུ་ཡོངས། (khyödh la ngedh pa rabhtoo yong,) you shall obntai much profit.

ཁྱོད་ངེད་ལ་དངུལ་ཇི་ཙམ་ཏེར། (khyödh ngedh la ngool jhitsam ter,) how may rupees will you give me?

ངེད་ཁྱོད་ལ་ལབ་ནི་མི་ནུས་ལགས། (ngedh khyödh la labh-ni mi nu la) I cannot speak with you.

ཅི་འཕྱིར་ཁྱོད་ངེད་ཚར་ཡོངས། (chi chhir khyödh ngedh tsar yong,) wherefore are you come to me.

ང་ཇི་ཙམ་ཁྱོད་འཚོའི་ཉམས་ཏུ་གནས། (nga jhitsam khyödhts; hoi nyamdhoo ne,) how long shall I remain with you?

ཞག་གསུམ་ངེད་དང་ཉམ་སུ་བཞུགས། (shagh soom ngedh dhang nyam soo shoo,) remain three days with me.

གང་ཞེས་ན་བཟང་པོ་ང་ཡང་སུ། (ghang she na sangpo nga yang soo,) who is the greatest among us?

ཁྱོད་ཡང་དེ་ལྟའི་བཟང་པོ་ཏེ། (khyödh yang dhe tai sang po te,) you are the greatest.

ཁང་འཚོ་འདི་ལས་མི་ནུས་སོ། (khongtsho di,) they cannot do this business.

ངེད་འདི་སེམས་མ་ཇེས་སོ། (ngedh di sem ma jhe so,) I have forbidden them.

ཁྱེད་ངེད་ལ་བདེན་པར་བཤད་ཡོང་ཏེ། (khyödh ngedh la den pa shedh jodh te,) you tell me the truth.

ཡང་ཅར་ང་ཡང་ཁྱོད་ལ་བདེན་པར་བཤད་ན་བསམ། (yang char nga yang khyödh la den be shedhna sam,) and I tell you the truth.

ཁྱོད་འཕྱུག་པོ་ཡོང་ལབ་ཆེ། (khyödh chhooghpo gödh le chte,) you will become rich.

ངེད་གཅིག་མཐོང་བ། (ngedh chigh dhong wa), I have seen one.

འདེད་མཁན་གཅིག་བཏིང་ལ་ཡོངས་འདུག། (dedh-khen chigh tingla young doogh), a sower went to sow his seed.

ཡང་ཅར་གང་རིའི་རྡོ་འགྲིལ་བྱུང་། (yangchar ghangchü do dil jhoong), and some fell upon a rock.

ཡང་ཅར་འདིའི་ནོ་བོ་ལ་འདི་ཉིད་འདྲིག་དང་། (yang char di-i no-oo la di nyidh di dhang,) and his brother asked him.

གང་འཕྱིར་དོན་ཁྱོད་འདི་ལྟའི་ལས་བྱས་སོ། (ghang-chhir dhön khyödh ditai le jheso), wherefore have you done such work.

ཁོང་ལན་ངའི་བཤད་པ། (khong lenngai shedh pa), he answered and said.

ཁྱོད་སུ་ཡིན། (khyödh loo gin), who are you?

ངེད་ཁྱོད་ཉིད་ཤེས་པ་མེད། (ngedh khyödh-nyidh she-pa medh), I dont know you.

ཕར་ཕྱིས་ངེད་ཀྱི་སར་ཉམ་དུ་མ་ཡོངས། (phar ghyi ngedh kyi sar-nyam-dhoo ma yong), be gone! Dont come near me.

ནམ་ཡོང་ཚེ། (nam yong tsche,) when you come.

དེ་ནས་ངེད་ཁྱོད་ངན་སྨྲས་བཏང་ཡོང་། (dhe ne ngedh khyödh la ngen mre tang-yong,) then I will give you plenty of abuse.

དེ་ཚོའི་ངེ་དེ་ཏ་བཤད། (dhe tshoi nge dhe ta shedh), his mother said to him.

གང་ཏར་ལང་པ་ཁྱོད་ངེད་ལ་འདི་ལྟའི་སྡུག་བསྔལ་བྱས་སོ། (ghangtarlang-pa-khyödh ngedh la di tai dooghngel jheso), wherefore have you given us such trouble.

ཁྱོད་རང་ཕ་མ་ཡང་ཅར་ངའི་ཉིད་ཚོའི་ཞིབ་གཟིགས་སྐབས་སུ་ཏེ། (khyödh rang pha ma yang char ngei nyidhtshoi shibhsi kabhsode), thy father and I have sought thee.

དེ་ཏི་དེ་ཡིན་བཤོད། (dhe-ti dhe yin shödh), he said unto them.

གང་ཁྱོད་ཉིད་རང་ཚོའི་ཞིབ་གཟིགས་སྐབས་སུ་ཏེ། (ghang khyödh nyidh rang tshoi shibhsi kabh soode), why did you seek me?

གང་ཁྱོད་མ་ཤེས་པའི་སྐབས་སུ་ཏེ། (ghang khyodh ma she-pei kabh soode), what did you not know.

ཁོངས་དེ་ཚོའི་ཉམས་དུ་འགྲོ་སོང་། (khong dhe tshoi nyam dhoo do song), he went with them.

ཡང་ཅར་དེ་ཚོའི་མི་ལ་གཏམ་འདི་བློ་ལ་ཞོག། (yang char dhe tshoi ma la tam di lo la shogh,) and his mother kept this word in mind.

ཁྱོད་ཉིད་ཚོར་ས་དཔེ་ཆ་གཅིག་བཏང་སྦྱིན། (khyödh nyidh tshor chhö pe chha chigh tang jin,) send me a book.

ད་ཚོ་ལ་དངོས་ངེད་ཀྱི་སྦྱིན་མཆོག། (dhe tsho la ngö ngedh kyi jin chhogh,) I will give you its price.

དེ་ནས་ངེད་ལ་ཡང་ཅར་ཁྱོད་ལ་དགའ་བ་ཡོངས་བས། (dhene ngedh la yang char khyödh la gawa yang wa,) then shall you and I be glad.

ནམ་ཁྱོད་ཕྱིར་ཡོངས་པ་ལས། (nam khyödh chhir yang pa le,) when you come back.

དེ་ནས་ཁྱོད་ལ་གཏཾ་སྙིང་བྱས་མཆོག། (dhe ne ngedh khyödh dhang tan nying jhe chhogh,) then I shall converse with you.

དེ་ནས་ཁྱོད་རབ་ཏུ་བགོད་བྲོ་བྱེད་ཡོངས། (dhe ne khyödh rabhtoo gödh dho jhedh yong,) then you will laugh very much.

ངེད་སྡིག་པ་བྱས་སོ། (nyedh digh pa jheso,) I have sinned.

ཁྱོད་ཀྱི་དག་པར་བྱེད་དགོས། (khyödh kyi dhagh par jhedhgo,) forgive me.

ངའི་དེ་ཚོ་ལྟ་བར་འགྲོ་བས་ཡོངས། (ngai dhe ts'ho tabhar dowe yong,) I am going to see them.

གཉིས་པར་བཤད་དང། (nyi par shedh dhang,) the second said.

གསུམ་པར་བཤད་དང། (soom par shedh dhang,) the third said.

ངའ་བུད་མེད་བྱས་ནས་ཡོད། (ngai bhir medh jhe ne yödh,) I have taken a wife.

འདི་ལྟང་ཏེ་ངའི་ཡོང་མི་ཐུབ། (dilang-te ngai yong mi thoobh,) therefore I cannot come.

ཁྲོམ་ལ་མྱུར་དུ་སོང། (thom la myoor dhoo song,) go quickly into the market.

མིག་མད་དེ་འདིར་ཁྲིད་ཤོག། (mighmedh dhedir theedh shogh,) bring the blind here.

ཁྱེད་རང་གང་བྱེད། or ཁྱེད་རང་ཅི་བྱེད། (chedh rang ghang jhedh khyedh rang chi jedh,) what are you doing?

ཁྱོད་རང་ལ་གང་དགོས། (khyödh rang la ghaug gö,) what do you wish for?